Little Sick Me

The Situations: Nice & Kind

Heather Ann Lynn

To order additional copies of this book, contact:
Xlibris
1-888-795-4274
www.Xlibris.com
Orders@Xlibris.com

ISBN: Softcover   978-1-9845-8348-2
        Hardcover   978-1-9845-8349-9
        EBook   978-1-9845-8347-5

Print information available on the last page

Rev. date: 06/12/2020

From the author, it is my deepest gratitude to be able to write a book about the nice and kind situations in my children's collection series. The books written and published are examples of exemplary behavior in families and the joy a team makes in their unit together.

With that being said, I dedicate this to my two loving boys, Bradley and Vincent. I hope that *Little Sick Me* will bring great memories now and later in our many fun routine living situations.

It is a changing time, Mom says, as the news plays loud and clear.

"COVID-19 is bad, and we're hunkered down, my dears."

Mom is cool, quick, and calm. She waves everything along.

Movies, slumber party cakes, and tea supplies–Mom whips up something very nice.

Keeping time and bumping tunes,
she finds a way to shake the room.

It's tough to find things barren. We make the most—let's keep sharing!

Stay safe! Stay safe! People wash their hands! This isn't no-man's-land!

Some may get sick, some may not. But I say we've got the best of luck.

Each and every time, Mom makes things OK.

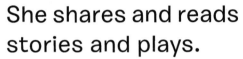

She shares and reads
stories and plays.

God bless Mom from the stars back to home. For we know who the true champion is at roam.

When she's not with us, she stakes out, tried and true. She wears her mask and covers her tracks. It's important to do these two.

Being careful, safe, and learning is the surely best thing. If we'd all stay healthy, we'll be sure to enjoy all of the little things.

Getting sick is no fun, and we would not want that to happen. It can be scary, frightening, or enlightening; but I'm not sure I like the fighting.

Our bodies fight when there's work to do. It makes us feel completely though.

When the sickness arrives, you know who you want by your bedside.

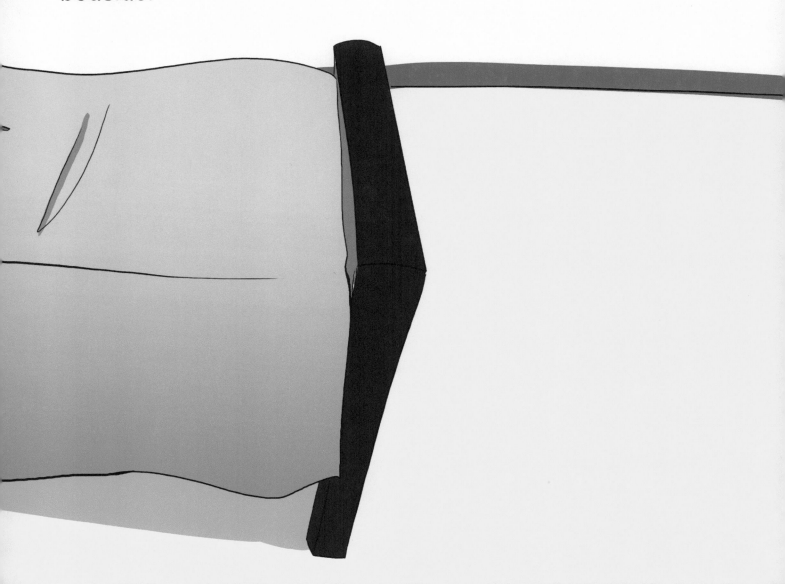

She is there—calm, collected, and sweet—in her mask and dressed from head to toe with white sheets.

About the Author

Heather Ann Lynn is a single mom of two young boys living in the suburbs of Frederick, Maryland. After years of hobby creative writing, baking confections, family, and making memories, it is now with great pleasure that she's publishing.

This is the second book of a series of five to be published for the surrounding community and the world to enjoy. Thank you!

CPSIA information can be obtained
at www.ICGtesting.com
Printed in the USA
BVHW022301270620
582394BV00015B/6

* 9 7 8 1 9 8 4 5 8 3 4 8 2 *